D0983535

Heart's Thread

Poetry Books by Livingston Rossmoor

A Stream Keeps Running (2013)

Do You Hear What I Sing (2014)

A Journey in the Animal Kingdom (2014)

A Never-Ending Battle (2015)

When Ruby was Still in My Arms (2015)

I Hear the Ocean Landing (2016)

The Thunder Was So Mad (2017)

I Found Ruth Tonight (2017)

Collected Triplets (2018)

Selected Ballads, Villanelles, Couplets,
Tanka Sequences, Cinquains & Triplets (2018)

Selected Sonnets (2018)

Selected Poems 2002-2017 (2018)

Heart's Thread (2020)

Heart's Thread

by Livingston Rossmoor

Published by
EGW Publishing
(since 1979)

I dedicate this book to
those in my memory and in
memory of my mother (1921-1953).

Thanks to Lisa Rigge, Charles Sandler,
Andy Shinkle and Chris Slaughter for
reviewing this book. I particularly wish to
thank Charles Sandler, Andy Shinkle and
Chris Slaughter for their help in restructuring
sections of this publication, and Chris Slaughter
for the organization and production of this book.

EGW Publishing (since 1979)

ISBN: 978-0-916393-45-8

www.egwpublishing.com

"Tis not the many oaths that make the truth;
but the plain single vow, that is vowed true."

William Shakespeare

"And you told me how bright the sun can be,
how hope can last beyond what we can see."

Livingston Rossmoor

TABLE OF CONTENTS

XIII   I Began to See and Touch, to Hear and Feel

XIV   The Ferryman

Postlude

PRELUDE

The Thunder Was so Mad

I was summoned and dispatched
to witness her demise
before the coffin was sealed.

He rented a truck to bring her back
to our home
down south.

In the rain, I heard the thunder,
the sky unhinged from the heavens,
angels shedding their tears.
The wipers could not keep up
with the emotional outbreak.

An old truck carried her coffin
in the drencher.
In the dusk, the lightning discharged,
a thunderbolt warning what was coming next.

The cannonade of
rock-breaking cacophony
twisted, manipulated,
tortured in hell,
the pain simmered,
the travail roiled,
teeth gnashed,
rage ruptured,
the sorrow burst,
the grind continued.

No one ever explained it to me;
"How can the sky be so angry?"
I was too small and too short
to reach the dashboard,
let alone to see what was ahead
or what was going on. I could only
gaze at the wipers and wonder
why the sky was being kicked out of the heavens.
Why the angels cried.
Why the lightning insisted on blazing with queer light.

The thunder was so mad
as though no one understood him.
A scream or yell was not
enough to proclaim his inner flame
agitated in the rain.

Since then, whenever I hear you,
I realize
you've never healed,
an ever-fracturing voice
that can neither express your
distress nor
untangle your torment.

Again and again,
you try to explain.

Heart's Thread

I
Stiff and Numb

A Remote Memory

So nice, the lunch you cooked to feed the homeless.
And I was not aware until decades after.
How small I was, naive and blind, I guess.
A memory, I still can hear the laughter.
Begging, drifting by the War, and thereafter.
I couldn't tell who was who, all strangers to me.
I was six, my younger brother was just three.

Pots and pans over the stacked bricks,
half-burnt twigs and sprigs jam the pit,
stoking the heaps of embers next to the creek.
Between the blocks, piles of dust and grit.
Due to the War, tramps, bums took a hard hit.
A shipwreck on the freezing sea, life-vests afloat,
near and far, distant from the sinking boat.

Stiff and Numb

Her transfusion was delayed on a weekend.
The operation failed, 10 years later, I was told.
Sorrowful voices, sorry faces, relatives, friends.
Routine surgery turned fatal, news became old,
the world moved on while I was on hold.
Waiting, waiting, maybe back, you would come.
Longing, longing, till cold, stiff and numb.

There's no one who dares to pursue or chase,
or taint the forthcoming shadow of the death.
And over the horizon, the approaching pace,
nearer still, holds and counts one's breath.
Heaven in its truth. Hell, frozen to the breadth.
The pain preempts the primal drear,
the tears confirming everyone's fear.

No One Knows

A Sunday school teacher, I was in your class.
Roman alphabet, pronunciation was rare.
They said you were in church or at the Mass.
I prayed, I looked, but you were not there.
And years, and years, I could not find you anywhere.
I felt, I heard, I swore; I pled on my knees.
I'm sure you're watching somewhere over me.

And no one knows the reason, or what's behind it.
Tumult tolerates strife, strife forgives friction,
friction bides in the never-ending brawl. Grit,
the last straw and the final conviction.
Wailing, tears subside, but not the affliction.
The signals are all fading, the loose,
fatigued eyesight hanging on a temporary truce.

Why No Answer

What? White flowers for kids whose mothers died.
The rest wore red to celebrate the Mother's Day.
Teacher's idea? School policy? First time I tried
to fight the rule; red and white all turned to gray.
A little boy coping to find his way.
But how to forget and where to go?
Why no answer, what else to know?

The fire has been extinguished for a while.
There are no embers left, nothing to strew,
to rekindle the spark, but the moan and bile
of lingering laments and effete view.
Ask the pounding waves, ask the blue.
The echo dissipates and the sound
subsides. Glistens darken, ashes on the ground.

It Never Would Be Me

A mother buttoned a coat over her son.
With hesitant and languid pace,
I was chilled behind the smiling one
and the worrisome mom who rubbed his face
and asked, "Are you cold?" with effortless grace.
Dying sun, fading autumn, let it be.
And shadows remain, it never would be me.

It finally surfaces, not in the laughter,
nor in the tears. It just emerges, used to hide
in the corner, on the perimeter after
bearing the inmost wound and ruinous pride.
There's no sheath to cache the scar and set aside.
Piling up, piling up, surfaces to the brink,
from the core of my being, it starts to sink.

I Wished I Was He

The graduating party from the high school,
in uniform, rigid and square in my seat,
a violin's sound from the stage, soft and cool,
reminiscence of the dream, no drum, no beat.
Romance no. 2 by Beethoven, what a feat.
Lessons since he was six, I wished I was he.
The romance, the warmth, it never would be me.

The moment never will arrive to
pity the search as no one feels the sting.
Why hesitate? Why wait for the clue?
It is embedded in every twine and string.
There's no sugar coating under the wring.
The cumulation of grief that gravitates
to nadir, simmers, quivers as it agitates.

II
I Should Hear the Ocean Landing

The Campus

The campus, the green, green rolling hill,
with classrooms around the grassy field,
and meadow over knoll amidst the birds' trill.
Lie down and roll; earth and heaven are our shield.
There is no freedom to declare, no cage to yield.
Walk, bike, candor and cheer, praise and no scoff.
With wings stretching, birds are eager to take off.

The lava impelled to transform to pupa, to
metamorphose to butterfly. In a hurry
to blazon their alluring dresses to strew
every spore and pollen in a flurry.
For the time being, no doubt or worry.
The glaring shine is the highlight of their prime
to testify a moment of truth that lasts a lifetime.

The Sky Is Not the Limit

Summertime, the aspirations ran wild,
endless assignments, bountiful wishes.
Around the lake, bank and bench, sunny and mild,
you came to share my reading. While breeze whishes
by the rowing boat and sleeping fishes.
And you told me how bright the sun can be,
how hope can last beyond what we can see.

The sky is not the limit, and there is no
heaven until the arrival of the heartbeat.
Soar, soar, above and beyond every foe
with daring and triumphant aerial feat.
Run, jump, no need to be pretty and neat.
Fly, fly, Livingston's seagull into the clouds,
resounds in the doldrums of the crowds.

Regardless of Where

Where reptiles' rustling feinted near and far,
the cafeteria quieted down in the night.
While frogs echoed and croaked under the star,
you came to visit me in the dim light,
the winds that blew under the moon, pale and white.
You smiled and told me you would be there,
when I sailed overseas regardless of where.

As the days went by, the travelers on the go,
bid good-bye and emigrate to
another coast, another tide, high and low.
The darkness calls through the morning dew,
searches and quests for the new from what we knew.
In the twilight's glow, the migrators roam,
through dreams and calls until they find home.

I Should Hear the Ocean Landing

The day to part the meadow, through the night,
you came to stay with me around the beach.
The sand that warmed my feet while you sat right
there next to me, the song you sang was a speech,
you told me and pointed at the stars I can reach,
and I would know someday, it's longstanding,
you said I should hear the ocean landing.

That loon's yodeling actualizes the longing
of the soul, in touch with abandoned dreams,
forsaken desires, a sense of belonging,
an echo of unyielding and wearied screams.
So far away, so nearby, in the lingering gleams,
"Where are you?" someone wails. "I am here,"
and you reply, "You'll hear and feel, loud and clear."

III
The Old, the New

Foreign Country

In a foreign country on my own.
A break from work, never was there a day.
Before daybreak, darkness permeated the zone.
The rain it rained, the storm it stormed, it's always gray.
The success smiled like the glitz of a ray,
and failure, a rotten egg. It's you
who clung with me to the finish line. It's you.

While saddled with the load, the weight is heavy.
The end is obscure, resistance is in vain.
The flood confronts the frail levee,
the search goes on, I slog along in the rain.
In the dark, ape up and crawl, get on the train,
ease off the nerves and grip, let it find its own pace,
run, run, forsake the despair to find a place.

The Gate

I graduated, one after another school.
One exam, two, three exams, I have passed.
A diploma is just paper, not a tool.
But what's next? You told me to stand fast,
a living is not a given as in the past.
A dream versus reality is a quantum leap,
calm and climb regardless how steep.

The gate isn't meant to suffocate the flow,
it opens and shuts the artery, not
latching nor locking can strike a blow,
dictate the tide or reverse the clot.
Step-by-step, I tie and retie the knot.
It's the way it is, the soaring bubble will
never reveal the cold and divulge the chill.

The Old, the New

Paper, paper, floating in the wind.
Another one searching for a desk to land.
To not be caught in a bind, I clear my mind.
But with new logic and rules, where did I stand?
Perplexed, confused, stranded in the sand,
with unthinkable longing, a distant goal,
the hopeless dream that takes a heavy toll.

It's the rhythm, it's the words in the line,
a rhyme to echo and the music to please
the old soul. It plants and sows the sign
of growing seeds of rosiness in the breeze.
But where is home? And where is peace and ease?
It's an accent to announce, an elation
to cheer the endeavor against the stagnation.

The Cause

And resistance never ceased to balk or pledge
the built-in reason twisted in the maze.
My brain-waves wavered towards the edge.
The old, the new, tried to clear up the haze,
but the conflicted report sank me in the craze.
Denial and refusal prompted me to pause.
A moment to reflect and search for the cause.

It's a pattern, it's a symbol, it's a dream.
An uproar to retreat, a constant pitch to
tune up the lasting drive and the scream
of scrounging that seeks what is overdue.
The head spins bewildered without a clue.
It's the rest, it's the gridlock, it's the meter
to denounce the babble and the teeter.

IV
How Can I Forget

How Can I Forget

And how can I forget those two-job years.
16 hours a day, Saturday, Sunday, every day.
I stood up to failure, swallowing my tears.
The glass ceiling forced me to find a way
to grind through the blockades with nerve and pray.
My pain you witnessed, my sweat and moil.
A humble soul that shattered in the toil.

Forgetting my lunch, I raced to second job.
I couldn't afford to punch the time card late;
"Two checks, next day, payday, I grin and throb.
At late supper break, I'll grab an extra plate."
Oh, how I remember my working man's fate.
The hanging moon at dawn, night behind the cloud.
Sow and plow, dig and till to make you proud.

I Was Alone to Carry the Torch

The factory's down and company ends.
One wish was burnt, another hope that came.
Rush, rush, candles burning on both ends,
always another mountain to climb and claim.
Alone was I to carry the torch and light the flame.
To bounce ideas, there's none; where to send my plea?
A sail faded into the sunset on the sea.

Trying to survive the blast, assault and strife,
collapsed buildings are beyond tally.
I'm determined to search for a new life,
flounder, cross the demolished alley,
run, run, through lagoon, mountain and valley,
to fight with all I have and all my might,
I strive to escape and evade this plight.

In solitude, I answer questions of my own,
while buoyed by success there and failure here.
The vision illusive, the path unknown.
In the uncharted sea, year after year,
the sail becomes a journey, no end is near.
While buried in the stormy night, cold and chill,
the boat resurfaces out of sheer will.

While voyaging through a sea of
isolation unforeseen, I blunder
into the immense whiteness, stumble and shove
my way through ensnared wonder.
In the muttering and rumbling thunder,
the hurricane explodes all day and night,
in the darkness, only despair and fright.

How Long Can This Go On

Dark, glow, dark, glow, how long can this go on?
Where is the hole? Pry, patch and go.
The fight moves on, the battle not won.
And on a sunny day, pick a field to sow,
the whispering breeze soothes the blow.
With endless hidden loads in the heavy dray,
due dates, deadlines, day after day,

The whistles in the air, dispels to chase,
to hunt and hound. The target is blear,
hits and misses in the frantic pace,
the focus is diffused, the eyes remain clear.
Refusing to live in fear, still I can hear
the misled voice stranded in the bay,
and the ire lingers every single day.

The Opportunity

The opportunity that missed and passed me by,
I'd rather look for an island to land,
a shore to dock, a kite to fly in the sky.
I'd rather tramp on the beach and in the sand,
tighten loose ends, sail to the promised land.
Reset the goal, the eye on the bigger thing,
the quotidian spiels have lost all their sting.

With wind-beaten and rain-soaked boat,
no more will I sail through every cove,
every bay with lump in my throat.
Diving for the pearls in the treasure trove,
I would rather be innocent as a dove.
While saturated in the sunset, I stow my net,
the seagulls soar, it must be quite a fete.

A Glimmer in Sight

It's like before, the frogs compose, try a new
piece, the same as years ago, unfinished flair
rehearsing every night, they pace their rhythm to
the raindrops. Opening night is up in the air,
the younger frogs still vie to get a share.
Keep tuning, varying older songs, never
changing, up there, dimming stars forever.

The brightest star twinkles throughout the sky.
While burning ashes cannot block the glow,
the glorious story captures everyone's eye.
Are we in the tunnel? No one dares to know.
The march is on, gusto crawls in on its toe.
The torch is lit, for now let there be light.
Sing, praise, through the clouds, there's a glimmer in sight.

V
Ups and Downs

Ups and Downs

On the day you picked, I reached the pinnacle.
Beyond any dream, I never could exceed it.
This only time, you stunned me with a miracle,
and euphoria exploded, the light was lit,
as usual, greed and crave not lessened a bit.
Go, go, a straight line up, no cushion, no hedge,
a steep slope down, cornered to the edge.

And thousands of eyeballs and hundreds of
binoculars aimed to catch my leap and dart.
In spite of bumps and cuts, push and shove,
living for the finish line regardless of the start.
Rain or shine, day after day, with all my heart.
The faster the thoroughbred runs, the race
dictates an endless breakneck chase.

Every Day on My Feet

The rewards embolden my confidence.
It's decades in the making, more than just and true.
Not an accident, it's proof, it's evidence.
The date unveiled, it's You, not out of the blue.
With overwhelming zest, all the way through,
dash and gallop, ride the drum beat,
no ebb, no fall back, every day on my feet.

I dream at night and reverie is my life,
with full steam and brio, I flap each wing
and heed every idea, the plans are rife.
Grass is greener over the fence, as they say;
advice, counsel, lessons, all words lose their way,
I hum so fast, I make myself dizzy.
Perching, resting, buzzing, forever busy.

An Instinct to Turn Those Earfuls to Vision

Jet, drone, scooter, touring cycle,
shoot a film, a director, a movie star.
Ruby, sapphire, a racing vehicle,
emerald, sapphire, an antique car,
scorching wind releases genie from the jar;
d'Yquem, Petrus, Latour, Mouton, all Premiere Cru.
Cognac, whiskey, single malt, the whole slew.

And to fulfill my impulses, I dash to,
or hurry back, as my mind is fickle.
To and fro, forward, backward, every clue,
every passing caprice, on call to stickle
and pursue the cues that come in a trickle.
An instinct to turn those earfuls to vision,
if I can avoid the looming collision.

Blaze Up

A flabbergasting moment, balloons are blown.
And showing off what they can be, takes no time.
It would never be repeated, I've already known.
Exalt, blaze up flashy shapes in their prime.
Bouncy, jumpy, urges and desires climb.
After the party, they fly into the sky.
Higher and higher, no time to bid good-bye.

In the kettle, boiling water starts to shout.
The higher the heat, the faster rumors fly,
all vying to escape the narrow spout.
The opening is tight and most are left to cry.
A warning sign before the tears run dry.
And vapors scream to chafe adoring throng,
who cut in the dance while music lasts too long.

I Continue to Remind, Never Cease

Before the sunrise, serene and still,
without any drill, the stage is set to nag,
to pick things apart, no song or trill,
no content, no meaning, just a drag,
there's nothing to brag about, always a snag.
Like a naysayer, a woodpecker has been
waking everyone up to tag on the din.

Never dawdle, I'm igneous to prove my point,
a bleak premonition, a perpetual knock
to please my soul. I poke and peek to join
the rap and strike a warning around the clock,
no shout, no non-sense, as if on the auction block.
When the night is tranquil and at peace,
I continue to remind, never cease.

Never Thought the Darkness Would Come so Soon

When wind is not behind my tail,
you witness my suffering and downfall,
lights went out, curtain dropped, I missed the trail.
Success fosters the frill until I hit the wall.
Failures quashed bonds and cut off every call.
In a heartbeat, the sun descended below high noon,
never thought the darkness would come so soon.

Still, the mind is bewitched to march
forward, un-afraid of the pines and aches,
setbacks and grudges, or the heat to parch
the lands, the tempest to uproot the stakes,
the trembles of the shocks and constant quakes.
In the dark, I strive to see, shrugging off the plight.
Awake in bed, searching for the remaining light.

In the End, like a Bullfrog

I am a great baritone or a bass,
or a double bass suits me quite well.
Acapella? I'm the accompanist, I pace
and thump a good tempo, anyone can tell.
Flow, rhythm, I may lament, but never yell.
Singing is my love, tenor is not my choice,
I prefer my deep and resonant voice.

But no one cherishes my low-tone croon through
the night. What they want is; mosquitos, just eat.
In the end, my legs, they bite and chew,
my body, cut and dissected, an outright cheat,
on the dinner table, an exquisite treat.
There is no question, we are owed an opening night.
I will continue to rehearse, it is my right.

No Shining Jewels or Gems

While under billowing sky, gust and blow,
the lute is fractured, rifts widen, thunder
in the distance echoes the agony and woe.
The lightning strikes the big old tree asunder,
the music stops, everything is going under.
Unmoved by breaking rattle and eerie sight,
the waves rile up another scare in the night.

There are no shining jewels or gems. Hunt no more,
time to go home. I turn off the lights on
the boat, check around, shut the cabin door,
cross the bar alone, bugles' blares are all gone.
You woke me up to see the light at dawn:
"Each struggle is a lesson to mold me
through the fire, into who I am meant to be."

Through the Sleet and Snow

When my sponge-like foot pads start to shrink,
tighten, expose the rim to grab ice, I know
winter is coming. Santa is calling, time to prink,
via Arctic to North Pole, through the sleet and snow.
Before Christmas, "Ho, Ho, Ho," earth does glow.
"Not a creature was stirring,"* all eyes so gay!
Witness the night before, I pull the sleigh.

Blasts, squalls, keep going, I dig through ice to
eat lichen, on my mettle, even baby deer
can run 90 minutes after birth. I am who
is chosen for the mission, year after year.
Santa, sleigh and I, smile and cheer.
I work the hardest, yet in the end, still
become meatballs and sausage on the grill.

*From "Twas the Night Before Christmas" by Clement Clark Moore

When I Bud and Sprout

In the spring, when I bud and sprout,
I am fresh and bright, breezes abound,
caressing every leaf. Beyond any doubt,
all my buddies shall always hang around.
Need help? No one will give me the runaround,
and I rack up the sun's blessings in its glow.
Like a persimmon, I feel secure to grow.

It is so sad to see leaves say good-bye,
one by one, they leave me alone in a big mess,
bare and naked, no place to hide when birds pry.
The winds split my affair with sprig, a big stress,
despite how pretty I was in my dress.
In the dirt, I begin to envisage my lot
and soon I'll be moldered into the rot.

What Can I Say, I Am Just a Glow Worm

("We are all worms. But I believe that I
am a glow worm." Winston Churchill.)

I live on the wall, and work in the dark,
on the cave ceiling with green-yellow light
hanging from the tip of my tail to spark.
They line up to gaze at my gleam in the night,
I just do my job, fright or no fright.
I'm proud to be a glow worm, even for just
three days, sparkling in the glory before I bust.

It's a hard job, less and less workers dare to
take the assignment, no one to blame.
Dangling upside down, staring at the ceiling through
the night requires faith, as it brings no fame.
It's just a fine precept, nothing to claim.
Moribund and frail in palsy, my back is sore,
though Churchill believed he was a glow worm, via lore.

Strayed Lamb

It would be a relief to be as timid as a lamb,
a strayed lamb needs a chief to lead the bloc.
Lowering my head in silence, how quiet I am,
laze and loaf, obtuse to dispute in the flock,
I track the one in front around the clock.
Before it's all gone, the judgement day will come.
Amidst the din, You said, it'll come, the march and drum.

It is such a comfort to break and drop,
and out of the zone of abysmal free fall.
A blessing to shirk the trap and plop,
like a dying fish untangled from the trawl.
In the sunlight, strayed lamb awaits the call,
tame and mellow in the meadow, finds a path
to shed and spurn the malice and wrath.

No Good-Bye

It's been half a century since you were gone.
Never had a chance to say good-bye.
Too young to know how. And time moved on,
so I wrote, I composed for you, no weep and cry.
Places I went, people I met, things I asked why;
lyrics, melodies, stories, news, good and bad,
long poems, short novels, happy and sad.

Inhale, exhale, the singing goes on,
according to its course. Throbbed by
rhythm; resonates, subsides and then is gone.
Your voice lingers on, encore with tears in my eyes.
Ironies and sighs, keep the spirit high,
without a vestige, the trace-less rhyme
remains in my soul for the longest time.

No Closure

A closure? What's in your mind at the last hour?
Facing the cruelty, how would your babies grow?
A good-bye? When everything turned sour?
Daunted, weary, gloomy and low, grief, untold woe.
No ending, no closure, only you know.
The thread, the heart's thread, will always be there.
Never let go, forever etched in my prayer.

I swim right through the strait and harbor my wrath
against the stream, the drift and furious wind.
I pray the route I choose is the truthful path.
No cheers or bugles, only thread and grind,
it's limpid even if I'm deaf or blind.
Leaving behind the raging and howling sea,
I trickle with the tides, murmur on eternal plea.

Despite All the Angst

I quit telling the stories and dropped my pen.
I stopped singing after recording them all.
I printed them out during peak season when
deadlines, due dates, drove me through the wall.
That was the end of my writing and I stalled.
It was you, I had exhausted all my wit.
It was you, the heart's thread with hope and grit.

The tent's roof and poles endured the strike,
in the storm, withstanding the blasting sand.
In reality, on one hand, it holds the spike,
regardless of the wind; on the other hand,
no desert, then no mirage, no stand
to waiver, despite angst throughout the plight,
the rusted nails impale and pierce to bite.

In the Late Misty Night

The moon is fading behind the clouds.
The street is dead, my car at a red light.
I have a minute to myself, quiet, no crowds,
the sky is waking and turning bright.
You witnessed my struggle and daily fight.
Same deserted street, same light, time to go home.
Kids asleep, among the mist and clouds, stars roam.

Eluding search beams from the lighthouse, I sneak
across the slushy sallow sands, hush my
melancholy tune and ignore a streak
of misfortune to land in the darkest sky.
The pounding waves silence every cry,
I shall bring my torch to kindle the flare,
with ultimate resolve to claim my fair share.

I Keep on Asking Why

You watched my grueling moonlight years.
Before dawn, go to work, moon is still up there.
I sweat through the day with grind and tears.
Moon to moon, rain or shine, lunch, dinner, where?
Coming home, moon hangs high, dew is in the air.
No time to hold my children, years have passed by,
I missed that chance, I keep on asking why.

And years and decades ago, I thought I was
an intrepid explorer, absolutely able
to withstand the mournful sea and cause
of swelling onus, deluded fantasy and fable.
While the rain and sunshine follow their timetable,
I should not interrupt the prayer,
I should wait till the drivel dried in the air.

VII
Angel Never Gets Any Rest

Spring, Summer, Winter and Fall

Splashing, splattering, a rocky road.
Pebbles dance along the streamlet on the way
down the falls. Angel takes the big load,
cooks and heats up the meals night and day.
While the river foams, children jump and play.
In the morning, wagon squeaks the same old tune,
running along, until we see the moon.

Canary lives to cheer for everyone,
and dies to guard the toiling miners.
A restless sentinel till work is done.
Sacrificing, they are diviners,
canaries, angels and Shriners,
in heaven, on earth, answer every call,
spring, summer, winter and fall.

Central to the Core

Dash, dash, there they go, keep them rushing on.
It must be super urgent, no minute can let go.
Wheels hum, horses neigh before the day is gone.
The rutted road, press on, no lament or woe.
The angel knits the nest and goes with the flow.
Humdrum and mundane, kids' daily chore.
Home sweet home, angel's love, central to the core.

As though the allegory needs no evidence
to boost its poignancy, it may be short
or long, but always sing with confidence,
a moment in life contrives to hold the fort.
On the road, in the air, sailing from port to port,
and oar after oar, lament or zest,
sink, float, pray for the best, nadir or crest.

Angel Never Gets Any Rest

The savory smell of spicy odors in the air,
bouquet lingers, shredded pork sizzles in
tiny anchovies and celery with a flair
of piquant scent, indulged by a yawn and grin.
Cucumber, yellow tail, salmon skin
and seaweed, miso soup on a cold night.
The sun retires, kitchen bathed in the faded light.

Pinch of pepper, scrambled egg, fried rice.
Swirling and flipping, stir-fry with savor,
tofu strips mixed in the hot spice,
zucchini and onion garners the flavor.
Her short spare ribs, teriyaki dish a life saver.
Mother, grandmother, and three kids left the nest.
Humming and baking, angel never gets any rest.

Buzzing like a Bee

All these flowers count on the bees to find
a match, and they expound requirement,
and grind pedantic details in his mind.
Endless requests delay his retirement.
Petals, sepals in their best attirement,
pollinating, matchmaking, a wedding spree,
gluttons for work, drone the news, that is the bee.

The sound of buzzing is a symbol
of tenacity. Never tired, it is
steadfast, angel bustling and nimble,
bunt and jostle the world to turn and whiz.
It's a godsend to take care of the home biz.
Gossip, rumors, so much on bee's wings.
The mission summons all his queens and kings.

VIII
Three Children

An Ironman

At Busselton, Australia, he fulfills his dream.
Swim, bike, run, sunrise to nightfall.
Wait and wait; dawn, dusk till the stars gleam,
an Ironman as they announce and call.
At the edge of the cliff, we stand firm and tall,
gaze at the Indian Ocean and inner soul,
near and far, all the way to the South Pole.

Violin, quartet, recall the orchestra day.
Clapped, cheered, tears in my eyes, I was there.
Go and catch the secret of life, smile and pray.
Bon voyage, bugle calls, say the prayer,
behold the sunlight and rainbow in the air.
Mile after mile, along the course, run and fly,
page after page, ocean, land and sky.

Without Her, I'd Still be There

The resolve broken, my will torn into pieces.
Day and night, in the cage, out of sight.
Sun can shine, winds can blow, turmoil never ceases.
Cling to the nook; sunrise, sunset, a daily rite.
Pill, pill, pill, dream shattered, awoke in a fright.
Ordeal, doubt, hell, edge, heading nowhere.
Sinking, quicksand, without her, I'd still be there.

Every traveler has their own destiny.
While every journey is unique and rare,
head to a higher ground, fly in harmony,
revel in the bliss beyond joy and flair.
Let her frolic, faith prevail in the blare,
as they forget their folly and blind spot,
you remind, blindness never relents its knot.

A Hidden Grace Exists at No Other Place

She made a living like me, a "two jobs life."
Hold the line, hang tough, biting chill to the bone.
Three kids, two jobs, hustle through the strife.
Wind blows, night's late, the seed has been sown.
It will grow while stirring up the moan and groan.
Tomorrow is another day, another night.
Impelled to march on, with or without light.

It was You who brought her near to me,
to fill the void of every missing hug.
Forty years, seedling grew to a tree.
A blessing to shake off the dust with a shrug.
It'll come, the love, the trust, a true plug.
While nurturing a shining smile on her face,
a hidden grace exists at no other place.

IX
The World Is Changing Fast

The World Is Changing Fast

The world is changing fast, from arrow, knife,
to bullet, bomb. Now, robot and nuclear.
Push the button, annihilation, a strife,
all vanished and gone, where is the warrior?
Where's my home? A flying kite may look easier,
when the line is twisted, impeding its flight,
it's an ark on the stormy sea, buoyed into the night.

Students on the street, parents with their newborn.
Shrapnel, ashes, scars and smoke.
Burnt, charred, raging fires, no place, no thorn.
Politicians gag the media, grunt and choke.
Philosophers calm the soul of every folk.
Confrontations, clashes and wound in the heart
nurse a temptation to ignite a new start.

Looking for Water in the Desert Is Not Bright

The recognition everyone is vying for,
so firm, so fragile; diffusion and division.
Distrustful and greedy, countries go to war.
Doubt and cheat flames the collision.
Relationships hinge on respect or derision.
A wolf, a tiger, bides their prey and plays tough.
What animal besides humans knows how to bluff?

Sun burnt, mind dizzied, to hail or not to hail?
Looking for water in the desert isn't bright.
And pushing to the limit is doomed to fail.
Who cares what is wrong and what is right?
Endless cages; how to break away from this plight?
I pray for an answer from the sky,
the blue remains mum, silent to my cry.

A Lion, the King of the Land

The king is I, the words ring through the dale.
Power is mine, I rule the land with my pride.
It could all boil down to a gruesome tale.
A private club with stringent rules to abide.
Scout and hunt, growl and grunt, patrol and stride.
The voice of my kingdom, I bellow and roar,
the crest of my command, that is what I live for.

Break bottles, cut ribbons, say the prayer.
A vagabond, a habit to make "the kill,"
while crowds applaud and bugles blare.
I share the prize with my pride, at my will.
This is my jungle, my routine dinner drill.
Stop daydreaming, there will never be a truce,
even all my bearings are turning loose.

A World of Farce

From the beginning, the finish line is clear.
The farce incites the masses, ever more
obstinate to moan, as though the end is near.
Closing in, the blast of chopper's roar,
near and far, the outcries blast and soar.
The mockery pretends to please the crowd.
The threats, the lies and bluffs are so loud.

Fingers pointing day and night, common sense
infringed, the gray is foul and odious.
Obscurity finds a lie to discard its fence,
drop its weapons, the obvious becomes dubious.
One foot in the grave, it is serious.
Deeper, deeper, they claimed "No one breaks the law."
Layer by layer, piles up to stick in my craw.

A World of Spiders

The multi-country endeavors, spiders build
networks, relentlessly linking their webs
to every continent, empire, trade and guild.
They evolve in each habitat, never ebb.
On the surface, it is just some blebs.
As they disguise, setup, ballast and dance,
breaking their trap, there is no chance.

A soft landing onto spiders' webs, they cast
the hunch, too comfortable to be true,
as prey jumbles in the mesh to their last
breath, tangled in their gunk and glue.
Who's who are all corralled in their zoo,
lasso and bola each new reception,
spiders digest and conceal each deception.

The Tidings

The tidings cause everyone to think and crave.
What is breaking? Fault, cleft, the breach is on.
Can anyone hear the crack out of the cave?
No signs of subsiding, eventide or dawn.
Can wisdom stifle the duel before peace is gone?
Again, the wicked affairs grab the headlines.
And distorted perceptions draw the red lines.

Time bombs waiting to explode, grim and grave.
And blabbering mouths belie this horrid claim.
Racing, racing, wave over wave over wave.
Staunch reality, enemies sharpening their aim.
Spin and twist, squirm and writhe, running out of blame.
When pressure is on, scapegoat after scapegoat,
the mounting evidence is up to my throat.

A World of Tigers

Attack is the only name of the game.
A matter of survival, defense is in vain.
The best deterrence is to frame
the rival, strike and drag them down the drain.
No compromise, just aggravate the strain and pain,
and never shun away from any woes,
plotting every fight against all foes.

There's no end, unless get caught in a zoo,
or in a circus, a clown in a parade,
or a mascot on the flag in the blue.
There is no end, life is nothing but a charade,
like a mask in the masquerade.
Remember amphitheater, glorious day?
There is no end, where is my next prey?

Invisible in the night, cold and stolid,
woodlands behind bushes, shadow and gloom.
The coming blow is massive and solid.
A plot, the night veil foreshadows the doom.
Vigilant, but nothing ready for the loom.
The silence heightens my focus to stare.
My blood is curdled by the shiver and scare.

Mute, quiet, I listen to the sounds of the hooves
far away, the darkness conceals the action.
Heavy and thick, it is there, not a spoof.
Dense and opaque, the blitz is gaining traction,
the clan, the gang, the whole entire faction.
The impulse is vacillating, numb and drear,
as night falls, the air is frozen with the fear.

A World of Foxes

As though intimidation needs to call
upon reinforcements, the bandit hides
behind the bushes, takes aim at the stall
of poultry, awaits the nightfall and bides.
"Blind to the crime, neck gets slit." The old guides
and warns their young, "It is a losing battle,
save the allegory, lost not in the prattle."

The agitated foxes collude in the dark,
while targets are asleep in a sweet dream,
their inscrutable trickeries coalesce and bark,
a ruse is bound to explode with a scream.
The night will end and the sun will unfold the scheme.
Staring, staring, eyes through a sprig of bush,
stalking, waiting, prey gets mauled, becomes mush.

Is the Beach Taking a Nap?

Over the hill, is the beach taking a nap?
The waves subside after debating out loud
about who can jump the highest and slap,
that never irritates the hanging cloud.
Somersault, aerial feats, in front of a crowd,
the day is ending, while birds fly home,
argue, debate, settle in a nearby dome.

The curlew's call is the fabric of a dream
"half spirit, half bird," the haunting call
loitering in the dusky twilight's gleam
and shimmering camp fire, as tides rise, tides fall.
Sedge slumbering as reptiles rustle and crawl
in the flower bed circling the gazebo,
while light fades over the lavabo.

A World of Locusts

I breed, I torment, there is no end.
I discreate, I embroil, there is no truce,
I wipe out all crops, I divide and rend.
I eat up everything in my way, a deuce?
A devil? Famine, death, that is how it goes.
I accept no plea, indulge just my greed.
There's absolutely nothing above my creed.

I am born to destroy and aggregate.
I tear things apart, I am born to inflame.
No apologies, no rues, never mitigate.
My right I claim, others I frame and blame.
Swarm and horde to capture what I aim.
Bible recorded, no shame, no guilt, let it be.
History paused while I am on my spree.

All Distorted

The nose is exaggerated, the brows
elongated, mouth distorted and face
full of wrinkles. The impression plows
to embed a warped mind in the chase.
I'd rather be a dove to end the race.
Staring at the nucleus, their grief is on fire.
Please, put out the fire, the fury and ire.

Overlapping and intertwining the real,
with the fake charade. All fraud and tangle
to beguile the soul that makes me feel
the pain, and compelled to choke and strangle,
while they feign all their strength to halt the wrangle.
No one notices the twist, all turn a blind eye
to the bewildered mind that keeps asking why.

X
One Thing Never Regret

A Volunteer

So little, so immaterial, a volunteer.
Who does it? Why do they do what they do?
And ask nothing in return, a new frontier.
One year, two, three, you carried me through.
Over 20 years, you showed me something true.
A life with meaning, new faces and souls.
Another world for the needy, the bell tolls.

The harmony is not only a blend
of tunes and sounds. The rhythm, the beat
and the feeling all have to agree to fend
and repel the clamor and boiling heat.
No life for those deserted on the street,
no longer just a matter of wrong or right,
when misery pierces through the shiver and blight.

One Thing Never Regret

A messenger of spirit, never misses the mark.
Resound, echo, the lesson is on.
While troubled and worried in the dark,
strive for revival of heart, no war to be won.
One thing never regret, life isn't wasted or gone.
You told me, "Keep your peace during the flight,
let the wind take you to a new height."

Released dove soothes the wearied soul,
enabling me to find the renewal
of conscience, trapped not in the flurried hole.
A stillness, no more hurried as usual.
The sick, the dead, the ending, so cruel.
The serenity of the innermost kind.
A companionship to share in the grind.

In My Dream and Reverie

When in doubt, there're times I thought to quit.
You told me, do not return to the old scheme,
it's simple to start; to carry on takes grit.
Never again to play the same theme,
leveraging the grudge to silence the scream.
Is honesty a nuisance? Asked by the soul.
Isn't it time to mend and restore, set a new goal?

It takes years, the build-up dominates
the discussion, never an easy task
to please and charm. The essence resonates,
twists, highlights the facade in the mask.
In my dream and reverie, to whom shall I ask?
To clear the blur etched in the fading light?
Distorted harmony seizes the new height.

A Rare Gleam of Hope

The muddy beauty contest will never end.
The wind that never stops blowing is a pain.
You told me to tighten the loose strand,
for the rain will never cease to rain.
While heaven refuses to let it go down the drain,
you showed me the hidden world where the sun glows,
the moon shines, a sound sleep wakened by the crows.

While sharpening the details, focused to quip
and whip up the ardor, kindle the spark,
audacity displays its unlimited grip,
announcing an unforgettable mark.
A rare gleam of hope rises like a soaring lark.
Worry, a driblet of raindrop, becomes a splash,
vanishing on the ground, leaves no trace in a flash.

XI
Eight Grandkids

Eight Grandkids

And who could predict what would happen next?
One after another, here they come.
While smiling in the sun, no one was vexed,
innocence never fades; some play the drum,
some mimic blues guitarists, pluck and strum.
A chance to redeem each two-job day
and the regret of missing the play.

The sun, repelled and rejected by the walls
of a maze, determined to penetrate through
the layers, focused on its pursuit, it crawls
to a new angle searching for another clue.
Hiding behind the clouds, hanging in the blue,
ready for one more conquest, the sun
prevails, gloriously bright, triumphantly won.

Without Any Purpose, They Laugh, They Cry

Birthday goodies, uniform, bat and baseball.
Sun is high, grass is green, the day is great.
No strikes or balls, they are little and small.
Runs, runs, all the way to home plate.
Soccer kids chase the ball, leads to the gate.
Whistle blows, popsicle time, far and nearby.
Without any purpose, they laugh, they cry.

Wind, the conductor, orchestrates by the chart.
No gusts, no howls, mutes the music quiet and still.
Hear with your eyes, the voice resonates from the heart.
Lyrics from heaven textured by timbre and thrill.
Waking up and it's there, requires no skill,
clouds gather layer by layer at the crack of dawn,
frost waited all night with sleepy eyes and yawn.

Or Do You Just Want to Paddle the Boat?

The style and etiquette, the fashion
and terroir. Minute changes unmask a history
of savor and taste. The culinary passion,
a calling beyond the tongue and eatery.
Ski any mountain, surf every sea in reverie.
While ripples fret and simmer, jump and slap,
ocean and sky are eager to join the clap.

Or do you just want to paddle the boat?
And throw your canteen as far as you can,
up and down the tides, and quietly float
while dozing in the sun, drifting with no plan.
Or you just want to hang out with the whole clan?
How you talk and laugh, I still remember,
birds migrate, back to school, come September.

Time Will Pass, They Will Grow

Lyrics, literature, music and opera.
Climb to the pinnacle, take off and fly.
The ultimate fiber of an era.
Dive the deepest, you can if you try.
Fly the highest, everyone yells aye.
Over the years and decades, wind will blow,
snow will fall, time will pass, they will grow.

Libretto forever arousing, never dull.
Sun, robe over gown, unveils its mist
on the florid stage that shades with hues and lull.
The baton at daybreak never misses the gist.
Our Pilot reveals the treasure on His list.
Hill stratum leads to the mountain-stage.
The puff of brume and nebulae conceals the mage.

The Rescue

Premature, complications, surgery
after surgery, how Max got through
his first two years was truly a mystery.
An ordeal, a miracle, an inspiration too.
You saved him by giving the doctor a clue.
A lifetime gyre in his first six years; to move,
to survive, to live, to remind and prove.

One day, it will be a new one, the shiver
will be gone, the pitches vibrate and oscillate,
liberating the echo with no more quiver,
and coasting like bubbles, float and jubilate.
Time will come, you said, it will percolate,
it will lift the benchmark, heighten the feat,
exceed the quota, the words will never cheat.

What Counts Is to Finish with a Glow

And then, another baby in peril.
Righting the ship before it sank, you were there.
Misdiagnosis, reaction was visceral,
it could have plunged us in the dark and scare.
Time, place and a star, lined up with a prayer.
You were there to avert the agony and blow.
You said "What counts is to finish with a glow."

When I was young, I was promised a place.
"Through layers of nebula in the sky,
I dream of soaring over the endless space,
beyond the sunshine and moonlight, I fly,
I run and stumble, you hear my cry.
Thunder, lightning, the sky turning black,
onward, onward, voices echo, never turn back."

XII
My Ordeal

My Ordeal

The quicksand is the only common thread
through the revolving door of torment. A maze
of very thin twines wriggle around each dread,
sunken wheeze and every hollow gaze.
An accident that turned my life into a craze.
Starry night, smiling moon, may shed some light;
in the gulch, quiver, shiver, no end in sight.

Ski cap, heavy scarf, frozen eye
and dry greetings to forsake any obligation.
"Do not bother me, do not ask me why."
Every footprint is a precarious navigation.
Heart, guts, brain, all collapsed in aggregation.
In the same nook, I stare at the rusty crate,
dodge the glance of dagger from every fate.

The Edge

While curling up at night with shattered dream,
hazy guise, bewildered face, build up a defense.
Success, achievement, a wrecked scheme,
a fuzzy gaze ensconced behind every fence.
While heart-beats stop and start, I lose my sense,
the bonds burst, spiraling out of order,
edges rupture, floods engulf every border.

The light will shine, sun will rise and sun will set.
One day at a time to dissolve the clot.
Stars will glisten, moon will hide and moon will fret.
No one trusts the pledge, it is just a plot.
It comes to a halt, faints and fails on the spot,
to my knees, I knew the end was near,
at the River Styx, your voice, I could hear.

In Doubt

In the darkest storm, the boat was out of sight,
swallowing waves beyond any vessel could bear.
A small boat adrift on the sea, a broken kite
lost in the wind; roars, howls in the air.
I heard your voice, I heard the prayer,
while hurricane and tempest raged all
night and day to aggravate the bawl.

It's a battle to cling to the boat,
and sustain the failing struggle. There is no shore,
nor harbor in sight, nothing's afloat.
It is cold to the core; stiff and sore,
tell me, tell me, how to hold onto the oar.
The time bomb explodes on time, tear and rend,
will I be fighting alone towards the end?

The Hell

While through the gate, the human soul was sent to hell,
the anima confronts the shadow of sword
every day, enshrouded under siege and yell,
slashing, slicing, averting the stab in the horde,
bending, budging the blade that cut the cord.
The eternal moments, they all "come and go:"
Hades, heaven, the judgement, only You know.

Jangles, wrangles, there is no place to hide.
The combat drains the fleeting soul,
travail, sulk in pain, no dignity, no pride.
While fending off stiletto in the hole,
warding off the umbrage, pay the toll,
toilworn to hold onto a losing battle,
the stifled murmurs echo the death rattle.

XIII

I Began to See and Touch, to Hear and Feel

A Quest and a Vow

The ordeal torpedoed the heart and guts,
sent the ship to the deepest ocean,
unsettled the bearings with strokes and cuts.
Now, back from abyss, branded the marrow in devotion,
and stamped the skin that touched the roots of emotion.
A duel-job voyage fulfilled every toll,
from port to port, seaworthy as a whole.

Headwind or tailwind, the wounded soul
conveys the map of every previous wrest,
rebuilds the core and patches every hole,
avoiding all the missteps, a fresh zest
propels the vessel without any rest.
Repairs, amends, the ship is afloat now.
A clear calling, a quest and a vow.

I Began to See and Touch, to Hear and Feel

I used to hope for a rope thrown to me,
that would be the answer, all I need.
You sent a man to listen to my plea,
a stranger, a doctor of a rare breed,
he found a clue, while others took no heed.
Though the mental wound is harder to heal,
I began to see and touch, to hear and feel.

It is a protracted journey, the voice,
the trumpet, blare to rattle the cage.
A miracle, after no hope, no choice;
gleaming sun, blinking stars, it's more than a stage,
the breeze caresses the leaves, turns the page,
and takes its time to unlatch the rusted lock,
before long, caged birds fly beyond the rock.

Dampens Not the Valiant Buds in Bloom

You sent a teacher to tell me what to read.
While picking up the book, dice or no dice,
my pen started to sow the seed,
realign and revive as silence pays the price.
There's no need to be polite, neat and nice;
flatten the field, piece by piece, rate the merits,
polish the treasure, favor the favorites.

Destination is not the end of the street.
There's no hurry to fix the squeaky wheel.
Niche by niche, gap after gap, beat by beat,
fill the hole, pave the path, it is real.
It takes time to rekindle the ardor and zeal.
The premonition of the clouds and gloom
dampens not the valiant buds in bloom.

Trail the profile, the lines sharpen the angle,
and mesh the plane above the sphere.
Then chisel away with mallet to untangle
the queer vision until all is clear,
thus chip and twist, turn the fear to cheer.
After echoing the astute selection,
drum up the vigor to reflect the affection.

While mimicking the gesture and simper,
the similarity becomes a veil of mist
in the tiny beams to the pupils, whisper
the ulterior motive to clinch the gist,
solicit the virtue to exhaust the grist.
In the light, all burst to scrutinize and pry,
beyond analysis, a tear is in my eye.

Focus, Focus on One Thing Totally

Focus, focus on one thing totally.
I hang onto the rope, listen through the cloud,
while an urgent voice is needed vitally,
the message is clear and very loud;
keep a distance, no rush to join the crowd.
Heed the winds, swirl and blast near and far,
conflicted warnings and blessings, there are.

Spin and circle around the spiral spindle,
the gyration and whirling never owe
anyone an apology, they're ready to rekindle
the cinders, gear up to another glow.
The endless blows were all I used to know.
Focus, focus, the loudest thrum carries the clout.
Your fervid guidance removes every doubt.

Hurry, Hurry, Embark on the True Path

You sent an angel to wake me up,
"Hurry, hurry, embark on the true path."
It is neither a mirage, nor the cup
of despair, not as subtle or striking as Plath,
not a bubble nor a shadow in its wrath.
Roused from reverie with faith and trust,
at the end, ashes to ashes, dust to dust.

Once a coy, fainted heart, after facing all
adversity, the spine is firmed, a smile
emerges to cherish and welcome the small
wild flowers bidding their hello in style.
An honest simple soul, rid of any guile.
Looking up, looking down, heaven or hell.
A prayer to fend off the bullet and shell.

Follow the Angel Nearby to Seal the Gap

Is it an alley of no return? Or only
a part of the story? Absolutely no track
to trace, the path ahead is very lonely.
The layout is sketchy, there's no turning back.
Lighten up, thrust everything in my backpack.
Hidden answers are speckled all over the map,
follow the angel nearby to seal the gap.

The venture explores and breaks the new ground.
A beginning to proliferate and reach
the inner soul, shut off the rowdy sound.
The pledge is transparent, so is the preach,
keep quiet, abide the teaching, no screech.
An enlightenment deep in my heart
arouses the tinder, sparks a new start.

One Day It Comes Back

One day it comes back, the voice, the calling,
drip by drip, like a spring, trickle and bubble
again in a dry well. The appalling
clot dissolved, picking up pieces in the rubble,
while the uproar, dying down, so is hubble.
Such elegance, the arbiter of destiny.
Agony yields to a feeling of harmony.

It's been a long time since I could hear
the trills and twitters rustling in the breeze,
the melody humming in my ear,
and sense the wrinkles smiling at ease.
One day, no more dilemma, inner peace
blessed in His serenity, humble and proud,
I whisper a prayer to the Pilot out loud.

XIV
The Ferryman

The Ferryman

Queer, bumpy, rugged road to the ferryman.
Charon refused my coin, there's hope, still.
The moon was pale and white, stars were wan.
River Styx rushed through the gap over the hill.
The punishment sagged my heart, cold and chill.
Tight canyon, deep gorge, flowers drooped and dead,
inched sideways back, I held onto my heart's thread.

When unconscious on the ground, siren's wailing,
time again, denial, dismissal, how to face?
Stopped beating at will, my heart was failing,
panicking, anxious in this life and death race.
Who to turn to? Pray for mercy and grace.
"Where is my Mom?" I asked, Holy Mother's voice:
"She's in my kitchen." that cemented my choice.

The Kitchen

There'll be a night when you come to comfort me.
No one sleeping in that bed, in the dim light,
you rush here, search there, where could I be?
You come back during the day, at midnight,
finding no breath, no vestige within your sight,
no more fight, I did all I could under the sun.
I know where to find you; I would crawl, I'd run.

In the clouds, a ladder and a rope,
through the window, I grab and I climb,
step-by-step, overcoming the steepest slope,
holding tight in the air, in any gust or clime.
Swinging through forests, climbing mountains, it's time
for the last journey; up, up, not a dream,
it's a thread, a plan; keep quiet, don't scream.

Fly, fly, holding onto the endless steps,
under gazing stars, over halcyon sea,
childhood, prime, old and sick, all for these preps.
Knowing where to go is music to my plea;
But rain, storms, whirl a melancholy key
over cliffs and pinnacles linked by hanging bridges.
Resolutely I navigate through the sharp ridges.

The gut, the will, the faith never dies.
Travail, hardship, a soft landing is my prayer.
Flowers in the garden, birds fly through the skies.
Nectar, tree sap, hummingbirds buzz here and there,
fragrance permeates, your smell is the air.
I make my way to the kitchen, my destination,
I wait and soak in your fascination.

This Time

Hair, the same hair, same as my only picture.
Through the bay window, silhouette of your face
bursts my reminiscing with no stricture.
Eyebrows, edge of mouth, rekindle every trace
of my dream; rattle every thread of inner space.
Then you turn around and walk to the grill,
closing in, that eternal moment holds me still.

The image of how you held the pot, the wok,
the spatula in your right hand; left hand with pan.
I was six, you were thirty-two, the clock
freezes the ravenous longing of a life span.
A familiar and heavenly smell, I can
begin to imagine what you would say:
"Come my son, this time stay and pray."

POSTLUDE

Mending His Net

Acapella or a violin's vibrato,
duet, trio, in parody or rhapsody,
he breathes fast to level the staccato,
smooth as a harmonious melody,
a poem jibing the syntax and prosody,
a sail boat fading in the sunset,
an elder fisherman mending his net.

Near sunset, he buries both feet in the dry sand,
the grains trickle between every bare toe.
Jogging alone with sandals in his hand,
in the morning, up before the rooster's crow,
along the shore, deep breath, lets it all go.
While early birds chase after the receding tide,
ripples efface stipples before the sand is dried.

About the Author

This is Livingston Rossmoor's 16th book. As of 2020, he has written and published 13 poetry books. His poems have appeared in numerous publications: local newspapers, magazines, newsletters and overseas publications. In addition, Livingston's poems have been published in *Leaves-of-Ink*, *Poetry Quarterly* and *The Lyric*. He has also written 2 books of prose and poetry, 1 book of 13 short stories and composed 21 lyrics and melodies collected in 2 DVD's and 1 CD.

Over his 40 year career in publishing, Livingston oversaw the production of 12 printed consumer magazines. He formerly served as the editorial director of the journal: *Nourish-Poetry* and is an associate member of the Academy of American Poets.

Livingston currently resides in California with his dear wife of 47 years. He has 3 children and 8 grandchildren.

176

CPSIA information can be obtained
at www.ICGtesting.com
Printed in the USA
BVHW031959040320
574116BV00001B/1/J

9 780916 393458